Gordon England's
Great Western Steam Album

Compiled by R.J. Blenkinsop

Oxford Publishing Co.

PREFACE

It was inevitable that I would acquire a keen interest in steam engines. My father had been following and watching traction engines and steam ploughs all his life, and my elder brother was already photographing trains when I was given my first camera in 1949 at the age of seven. My collection of railway photographs had started.

After sometime, and having compared my pictures with those taken by my brother Brian and other experts, I started saving for a better camera. In 1958, I purchased a second-hand Agfa Record 111, a 120 folding camera, which produced better pictures but sadly had a maximum shutter speed of 1/250th of a second.

All the photographs in this book, up to March 1960, were taken on this camera and it is obvious in a number of the pictures that to compensate for the slow shutter speed one had to take fast moving trains further way to avoid having a blurred front end. In March 1960, I was fortunate to acquire the ex Zeiss Miroflex camera modified by Dick Blenkinsop. This was originally a 9 × 12 plate camera but had been adapted to take 120 roll film. With a maximum of 1/2000th of a second shutter speed, and even with the fastest trains, providing one pressed the shutter release button at the exact moment, one could fill the negative.

Being born and brought up in Stratford-upon-Avon, most of my school-days were spent within cycling distance of the Western Region with occasional visits to the Lickey Incline to see *Big Bertha*, or to Rugby to see 'Duchesses' and 'Princess Royals'.

The opportunity to travel further afield came when I joined British Railways, on leaving school in 1957, as a junior clerk at Stratford-upon-Avon goods depot. The goods yard was the happiest place in which I ever worked, where every member of the staff was a character — Fred, Charlie, Nobby, etc. All worked as a team and worked hard, yet there was so much fun, with a lot of practical joking, and the majority really enjoyed going to work. There were no thoughts of redundancy or unemployment (Dr Beeching had not yet been appointed) and I felt that this was perhaps how the yard had operated for close on one hundred years. As a railway friend said to me the other day; 'In those days we worked hard and got the work done but had such fun — now you don't know what is going to happen from day to day'.

I was lucky not to be caught during my regular disappearing acts from the yard to see *Tenby Castle* on the 'down' 'Cornishman', a clean 28XX on a freight, or a special excursion, and good old Harry in the office covered up for me no end of times.

Allocated to the top of the yard was a Collett 0-6-0 22XX class for shunting duties and also to assist trains up the 1 in 75 incline to Wilmcote, and it was always exciting to be on the footplate blasting up the bank on the back of a heavy freight train. On one such ride we unexpectedly had to bank a train all the way to Earlswood and run back tender first (approximately a 26 miles round trip). Imagine walking back into the office after about an hour trying to pretend I had difficulty finding a particular wagon in the yard. I was soaked, filthy and covered in coal dust from our tender-first ride home!

Full use was made of free passes and privilege tickets to reach such places like Beattock, Dainton, Grantham, Bath, etc. The whole system was now within economical travelling distance and, in possession of two free passes to both Inverness and Penzance, one had a great choice of places to visit.

A typical trip would be to travel down on Friday night to Newton Abbot arriving at 04.40 on Saturday. Then a brisk walk up to Dainton Tunnel making full use of the photographic walking permit.

After a day with double-headed 'Kings' and 'Castles', and with plenty of film left it was out with the timetable to find a slow train heading north on which I could enjoy some overnight sleep. Shrewsbury was chosen and, after collecting some more shots on the Sunday, a quick look round the shed and it was back home, tired and hungry. Oh dear, they have forgotten to cancel my tickets — should I risk going back on another occasion to get my ticket punched!

My interest was to get out in the countryside to watch steam engines hard at work and, at that time, I never dreamt that one day the photographs taken would appear in a book. This book contains a selection of Western Region photographs and brings back many happy memories for me.

I owe a great deal of thanks to Dick Blenkinsop for selecting and printing the negatives and compiling the book for, if it was not for him, most of these pictures would never see the light of day.

A FOULIS-OPC Railway Book

© 1987 R.J. Blenkinsop, G. England & Haynes Publishing Group

Reprinted 1988

Published by:
Haynes Publishing Group
Sparkford, Near Yeovil, Somerset. BA22 7JJ

Haynes Publication Inc.
861 Lawrence Drive, Newbury Park, California 91320, USA

British Library Cataloging in Publication Data
England, Gordon
 Gordon England's Great Western steam album
 1. Great Western Railway 2. Locomotives—England—History
 I. Title II. Blenkinsop, R.J.
 625.2'61'0942   TJ603.4.G72G73
 ISBN 0-86093-386-5

Library of Congress Catalog Card Number
87-82793

Plate 1 (Below): Collett 0-6-0 No. 2274 propels inspection saloon No. 80974 (now at Tyseley) over the Stratford-upon-Avon and Midland Junction Railway at Goldicote Cutting, near Ettington. No doubt the inspection staff were looking at the new junctions to be put in at Fenny Compton and Stratford-upon-Avon to enable the South Wales iron-ore trains to avoid the climb to Hatton on the main line. Normally, a nice clean engine was provided, but not so in this case. However, the coach appears to have been cleaned, with all the brass handles and hand rails well polished.

27th March 1958

Plate 2 (Above): A 4-4-0 locomotive, No. 9017, hauls the 'Severn Rambler' railtour over the Banbury to Cheltenham line and is seen on the long climb from Bourton on the Water to Notgrove Station. This was the highest through station on the Great Western (760ft. above sea level) and was the reward for a 78 mile cycle ride on the eve of my 16th birthday.

20th April 1958

Plate 3 (Below): After a hard and unsuccessful ride on to Cheltenham, in an attempt to take another picture of the train, there was just time to quickly look around the engine shed. Outside, 2-6-2T No. 5514 looked attractive in its newly-acquired green lined-out livery.

20th April 1958

Plate 4 (Above): A number of excursions ran to Stratford-upon-Avon during the summer months. This one is seen leaving for its return journey to Llanelly, behind No. 5961 *Toynbee Hall.*

21st May 1958

Plate 5 (Below): No. 7920 *Coney Hall* waits in the bay platform before departing from Stratford-upon-Avon with the 17.41 stopping train to Leamington Spa. This was a through working from Worcester who were responsible for the motive power, and occasionally had a clean engine normally reserved for the London trains.

21st May 1958

Plate 6: The 'Cambrian Coast Express' approaches Snow Hill Station, Birmingham, behind No. 7025 *Sudeley Castle*. At this time the locomotive was allocated to Old Oak Common (81A) but was later to be transferred to Worcester.

26th May 1958

Plate 7: BR 9F 2-10-0 No. 92222 had not been built long when it was photographed ambling down the line from Wilmcote to Stratford-upon-Avon with about 30 wagons of used ballast. Very few of these engines were kept clean, and one had to be lucky and photograph them shortly after leaving the Works.
13th June 1958

Plate 8 (Above): It was unusual to see a 'Grange' class locomotive carrying 'The Cornishman' headboard. In this case the train was running in two parts due to heavy summer traffic, and No. 6876 *Kingsland Grange* is seen leaving Stratford-upon-Avon with the first part, and with the usual 'Castle' class engine following on the main part.

13th June 1958

Plate 9 (Below): No. 6808 *Beenham Grange* and No. 7905 *Fowey Hall* make a spectacular ascent of Dainton Bank with the 'Cornish Riviera Express', having taken the train over at Newton Abbot from No. 6026 *King John*. These engines would be taking the train through to Penzance and the 'King' would be available to pilot the 10.35 Paddington to Plymouth train, also 'King'-hauled, so giving the railway photographer the opportunity of a lifetime.

21st June 1958

Plate 10 (Above): 'Britannia' Pacific No. 70019 *Lightning* heads a Paignton to Newcastle express along the sea wall at Teignmouth. The West of England saw some interesting workings in the busy summer season and on this occasion it is a Cardiff-based locomotive.

22nd June 1958

Plate 11 (Below): Having finished the short but very steep climb from Aller Junction, 2-6-2T No. 5158 and 2-6-0 No. 6354 emerge into the daylight from Dainton Tunnel with a train of empty milk tanks.

23rd June 1958

Plate 12 (Above): No. 4971 *Stanway Hall* heads a goods train round the sharp curve leading into Teignmouth Station and captures the attention of the holiday-makers who, judging by their clothes, were having a rather chilly time.

22nd June 1958

Plate 13 (Below): No. 7029 *Clun Castle* climbs the last few yards up to Dainton Tunnel with the 08.45 Plymouth to Kingswear train. *Clun Castle*, so well known today in preservation, was regularly seen hard at work on the South Devon banks as, at that time, it was shedded at Newton Abbot.

23rd June 1958

Plate 14 (Above): An 0-4-2T, No. 1466, hurries past Aller Junction with the 10.05 Paignton to Newton Abbot stopping train. The lines to the right are for Plymouth, and the start of the climb to Dainton. A 2-6-2T can be seen by the water column just beyond the junction waiting to bank the next freight train.
24th June 1958

Plate 15 (Below): An 0-6-0PT, No. 3659, hauls a short goods train towards Aller Junction, probably for Totnes. Note the double-decker bus on its way into Newton Abbot with all the ladies in their best hats!
24th June 1958

Plate 16: No. 4079 *Pendennis Castle* pilots No. 5011 *Tintagel Castle* past Aller Junction with the westbound 'Cornishman' from Wolverhampton. Again we have another bus in the picture, but this time a rather vintage single decker.

24th June 1958

Plate 17: With only nine coaches, this combination of 'Grange' power should have no difficulty on the gradients ahead after leaving Newton Abbot. No. 6805 *Broughton Grange* and No. 6842 *Nunhold Grange* have a Swansea to Penzance train, and it looks as if the local gangers have been at work with their scythes.

24th June 1958

Plate 18 (Above): It rained so hard nearly all day, and I could think of nowhere better to go than Totnes Station and shelter under the station canopy from where the 'up' 'Cornish Riviera Express' was photographed. No. 4098 *Kidwelly Castle* is piloting No. 6026 *King John* as they come through the station after the steep descent of Rattery Bank.

25th June 1958

Plate 19 (Below): During a brief pause in the rain, 0-4-2T No. 1472 is seen approaching Staverton Station with an Ashburton to Totnes train.

25th June 1958

Plate 20 (Above): A 2-6-2T, No. 4176, makes a fine picture as it approaches Dainton Tunnel with a westbound freight. Note the tarpaulin stretched over the wagon, and the No. 8 target number on the buffer beam.

Plate 21 (Below): No. 6010 *King Charles I* climbs up the 1 in 37 incline to the cutting before Dainton Tunnel with the 11.30 Paddington to Penzance express — note the selection of signals all in the 'off' position.

Plate 22: This was my favourite position on Dainton Bank where No. 5098 *Clifford Castle* is seen climbing out of the trees near Stoneycombe Quarry with the 'down' 'Royal Duchy'. During a week's holiday this was the only train that did not take a pilot engine at Newton Abbot. The absence of route reporting numbers, a nice headboard, and perfect exhaust makes this the shot of the week.

27th June 1958

Plate 23: How things had changed over the years when I went to this spot in 1985 to see one of the GW 150 specials — all overgrown and quite impossible to repeat a similar picture. No. 5920 *Wycliffe Hall* and No. 5073 *Blenheim* approach Dainton Tunnel with a Manchester to Penzance express.

28th June 1958

Plate 24 (Above): No. 4919 *Donnington Hall* and No. 7027 *Thornbury Castle* pass Stoneycombe sidings with the 08.25 Paddington to Penzance express. The fireman of the first engine seems to enjoy having his photograph taken and, judging by the exhaust, it looks as if the 'Castle' is doing most of the work.

28th June 1958

Plate 25 (Below): As I stand just opposite Dainton signal box, No. 6829 *Burmington Grange* and No. 4931 *Hanbury Hall* emerge from the tunnel with a train for Falmouth, and start the descent to Totnes. Note the delightful PW hut on the other side of the track, complete with its tall brick-built chimney.

28th June 1958

Plate 26: With the Great Western coaches now painted in maroon livery, No. 4083 *Abbotsbury Castle* comes out of the east portal of Dainton Tunnel with a train for Newton Abbot. Part of a railway photographer's nightmare, the telegraph poles and power lines, are very prominent in this shot.

Plate 27: In a marvellous rural scene, 2-8-0 No. 2809 comes very slowly up the bank with a long freight train, assisted at the rear by 2-6-2T No. 5154.
29th June 1958

Plate 28 (Above): For those of you who go to this location to see the current 'Sunday Luncheon' steam specials, this is how it used to look. A 2-8-0, No. 2870, in commendably clean condition, tops the climb out of Stratford-upon-Avon and approaches Wilmcote with a ballast train.

23rd August 1958

Plate 29 (Below): On summer Saturday evenings, Tyseley-based 2-6-0 Moguls were employed piloting the returning holiday traffic to the Midlands, on the section between Stratford-upon-Avon and Birmingham. Here No. 6307 is assisting No. 6803 *Bucklebury Grange* at Wilmcote with a train from Weston-super-Mare.

23rd August 1958

Plate 30 (Above): For many years No. 7007 *Great Western* was shedded at Worcester which was a good choice by the authorities as that shed always kept the 'Castles' in fine condition for the London trains. No. 7007 is seen on a rather dull day leaving Chipping Campden Tunnel.

31st August 1958

Plate 31 (Below): A 2-6-2T, No. 4156, assists 2-6-0 No. 6361 on an 'up' goods train, shortly after leaving the Severn Tunnel. The pilot engine would have worked all the way through the tunnel from Severn Tunnel Junction, on the west side of the river.

6th September 1958

Plate 32 (Above): The Stephenson Locomotive Society organised a railtour to Swindon from Birmingham, and here the train can be seen in the platform on the left of the picture. While the passengers were looking round Gloucester running shed, the locomotive, No. 4900 *Saint Martin*, was taking on water. This was among its last passenger duties, and it was withdrawn from service in the April of the following year.

7th September 1958

Plate 33 (Below): A 2-6-2T, No. 4161, stands outside the ex-GWR shed at Stratford-upon-Avon. The wagon body behind the water column was the foreman's office occupied at that time by a Mr Tom Duckett. The line in the foreground had not long been laid, to provide extra capacity for the London Midland engines which had to be housed there following the closure of the old shed at the Town Station. Initially, there was a lot of argument as to who's engines should go in at night!

20th September 1958

Plate 34 (Above): Bentley Heath is the location for this picture, which shows No. 5040 *Stokesay Castle* with the 'down' 'Cambrian Coast Express'. The level crossing can be picked out just beyond the overbridge, and I always had a soft spot for this engine so the chimney graces my lounge as a rather heavy coffee table.

4th October 1958

Plate 35 (Below): Approaching the crossing as seen from the footbridge in the last picture is No. 5046 *Earl Cawdor* and No. 5088 *Llanthony Abbey* with the 11.10 Paddington to Birkenhead express. Both pictures have been made by the lovely brilliant autumn sky.

4th October 1958

Plate 36: A busy Sunday morning at Swindon, following an accident involving 2-8-0 No. 4707, 2-10-0 No. 92003 and No. 5009 *Shrewsbury Castle*. One gang are busy restoring the main line, while others are lifting off the connecting rods, and No. 6942 *Eshton Hall* and 2-8-0 No. 2835 are waiting to assist. The power of the impact can be clearly seen by the damage to the wagons.

16th November 1958

Plate 37: Inside 'A' Shop, at Swindon Works, No. 4950 *Patshull Hall* and No. 4086 *Builth Castle* look almost ready to leave after overhaul. On the right can be seen 2-10-0 No. 92201, being built new alongside a new 'Western' class diesel-hydraulic locomotive.

16th November 1958

Plate 38 (Above): On a cold January Sunday morning, 4-4-0 No. 9013 had just arrived on to the triangle at Swindon following its withdrawal from service a month earlier. From here it will be transferred to the Concentration Yard and to 'C' Shop for cutting up. Some of the other engines in the line await the same fate.

11th January 1959

Plate 39 (Below): A 2-8-0, No. 2801, has just arrived at Swindon from Pontypool Road Shed following what appears to be a bad accident to the cab and boiler fittings. It is seen outside the Stock Shed awaiting scrap. In the foreground, the late Tom Williams has obviously just taken his photograph and is winding on the film in his camera.

22nd March 1959

Plate 42: Swindon-based 0-6-0ST No. 1365 has just worked a Rail Enthusiasts' Special over the Uffington to Challow branch and, after running round its coaches, poses for photographs in Faringdon Station. The line has long-since been taken up, and the site developed into an industrial estate, but the station building remains now used by a company of funeral directors.

26th April 1959

Plate 43: With quite a gathering of holiday-makers on the beach, No. 7025 *Sudeley Castle* climbs away from Goodrington Sands with the 10.15 Paddington to Kingswear train.

20th June 1959

Plate 44 (Above): No. 5092 *Tresco Abbey* coasts down the grade from Churston past Waterside Camp caravan and camping site. I enjoyed several holidays on this camp with my parents and they never worried about me getting into difficulties in the sea, as I spent all my time by the railway line. This train is the 15.20 from Kingswear to Paddington.

20th June 1959

Plate 45 (Below): With a Newton Abbot to Kingswear train 2-6-2T No. 5158 rounds the curve and into Churston Station. The branch to Brixham goes off to the right. The grass on the embankments was cut regularly to reduce the fire risk from engine sparks, and this kept the lineside very tidy with conifers planted to improve things further.

20th June 1959

Plate 46 (Above): Whilst walking back to the caravan site after a tiring day, I paused at Churston Viaduct to see No. 5929 *Hanham Hall* hauling the 15.50 Paddington to Kingswear train. Only after processing the pictures did I notice the open door in the centre of the train.

20th June 1959

Plate 47 (Below): A 2-6-2T, No. 4117, crosses Greenway Viaduct with a stopping train from Kingswear to Newton Abbot. This scene has changed very little, and steam trains, operated by the Torbay Steam Railway, cross this viaduct throughout the summer season.

24th June 1959

Plate 48: With a goodly selection of signals, and also Great Western coaches, 2-6-2T No. 6119 pulls away from Paignton with a local train for Kingswear.

25th June 1959

Plate 49: No. 7029 *Clun Castle* and 2-6-2T No. 4176 are seen leaving Churston Station with the 10.20 Kingswear to Liverpool train. No. 7031 *Cromwell's Castle* stands in the station having just arrived with a three-coach stopping train. In the bay platform, 0-4-2T No. 1452 with an auto car are waiting to take passengers down the branch to Brixham.

26th June 1959

Plate 50: Later in the day, 0-4-2T No. 1452 propels its auto car, No. W224W, into Churston with a light load of two passengers.

26th June 1959

Plate 51: No. 6016 *King Edward V* has just arrived at Paignton with an excursion from Torrington, near Barnstaple, and is seen returning to Newton Abbot together with 2-6-2T No. 4105. The excursion returned in the hands of SR Bulleid Pacific No. 34033, piloted by 2-6-2T No. 5178.

26th June 1959

Plate 52 (Above): To mark the centenary of Moor Street Station, Birmingham, the Stephenson Locomotive Society ran a special train from Birmingham to Henley in Arden Old Station, via Hatton North Junction, and the Bearley North Curve. Here, 0-6-2T No. 6694 is seen coming off the curve to join the Stratford-upon-Avon line to Birmingham, just south of the Bearley Aqueduct.
1st July 1959

Plate 53 (Below): No. 7811 *Dunley Manor* pulls away from Cemmaes Road Station and starts the climb to Talerddig Summit. Note the cover over the signal wire to prevent the gangers from falling over.
28th July 1959

Plate 54 (Above): No. 6018 *King Henry VI* pilots No. D601 *Ark Royal* on the 10.35 Paddington to Penzance, and is passing Stoneycombe Quarry on the climb to Dainton. I went down to Devon particularly to see this sight as it should have had two 'Kings' as motive power which I mentioned in the caption to *Plate 9*. Perhaps, looking back now, the combination of steam and diesel is more interesting.

1st August 1959

Plate 55 (Below): A 2-8-0, No. 3802, coasts down from Dainton Tunnel with a Newquay to Cardiff train, emphasising the shortage of locomotives in the summer and the variety of workings which took place. No. 3802 was shedded at Oxley, Wolverhampton and was a long way from home.

1st August 1959

Plate 56: With an excursion from Ashley Hill, Bristol, 2-8-0 No. 4704 climbs up to Dainton Tunnel on what must have been a pretty hot day judging by the number of passengers looking out of the windows, or was it standing room only?

Plate 57: Those two splendid signal gantries stand guard over the approach to Newton Abbot for 'up' trains, as No. 4936 *Kinlet Hall* and No. 1021 *County of Montgomery* leave with a Manchester to Penzance train. The whistle is blowing on the leading engine and note how, with the sun head-on, much of the motion is lost in the black shadows.

29th August 1959

Plate 58: In the evening sun, 2-8-0 No. 4706 heads for Paignton having just come out of Newton Abbot Station round the corner. It rather looks like a set of sleeping cars behind the engine, so perhaps after turning, it would return to London in the middle of the night.

29th August 1959

Plate 59 (Below): Now we are back in the Midlands, and No. 7908 *Henshall Hall* and BR Standard Class 5 No. 73090 have just passed through Lapworth Station with a train from Pembroke Dock to Wolverhampton, made up with a nice set of GWR coaches. The relief lines on the right of the picture have, of course, now been taken up.

5th September 1959

Plate 60: 'Dukedogs' Nos. 9004 and 9014 head the Talyllyn Railway special train past Abermule Station. Both engines had been specially prepared by the staff at Shrewsbury Shed for this big occasion, but shortly afterwards they were put into store at Wellington Shed, and within twelve months were withdrawn.

26th September 1959

Plate 61: Some miles further on, the train climbs up into the Welsh hills and here it is passing Pontdolgoch Station with, even at that time, a tidy goods yard, although I doubt if it received much traffic.

26th September 1959

Plate 62 (Above): No. 5089 **Westminster Abbey** coasts down from the short tunnel near Cheltenham Racecourse with the 'down' 'Cornishman'. The track bed is still intact and the Gloucester & Warwickshire Railway plan to relay track on this section.

9th January 1960

Plate 63 (Below): With a football excursion train from Plymouth to West Bromwich, No. 5098 **Clifford Castle** produces a useful smoke effect in the low winter sunshine as it climbs out of Cheltenham. Only the road bridge to Swindon Village separates this photograph and the previous picture.

9th January 1960

Plate 64: Another picture taken inside 'A' Shop at Swindon Works, and this shows the last steam locomotive to be built by British Railways nearing completion. No. 92220, to be named *Evening Star* on 18th March 1960, stands alongside sister engine No. 92219.

17th January 1960

Plate 65: This photograph will be enjoyed by the preservationists at Didcot who last year restored this engine to its former glory. The 2-8-0, No. 3822, passes Chipping Campden signal box with an 'up' freight on the Worcester to Oxford line.

20th February 1960

Plate 66: The next two photographs were taken on the Stratford-upon-Avon to Honeybourne section, most of which has now been lifted. A 2-6-2T, No. 4109, crosses the River Avon near the racecourse with the 13.47 train from Stratford-upon-Avon to Worcester. Note the unusual form of bridge construction.

24th March 1960

Plate 67: Further on down the line is Milcote Station, complete with standard Fordson and threshing machine waiting at the level crossing. No. 4113 leaves with a local stopping train to Worcester. The request smoke effect did not appear to work very well!

7th April 1960

Plate 68 (Above): An 0-4-2T, No. 1409, and 0-6-0PT No. 8720 stand outside Wolverhampton (Stafford Road) Shed. The locomotive on the turntable had been repainted in plain green livery and, half the coal loaded went on the cab roof or on the ground behind the engine!

24th April 1960

Plate 69 (Below): An interesting view of 2-6-2T No. 6112 just nearing the end of an overhaul in Wolverhampton Works. Note all the line-shafting in the background for driving the machine shop, and the various parts scattered over the floor.

24th April 1960

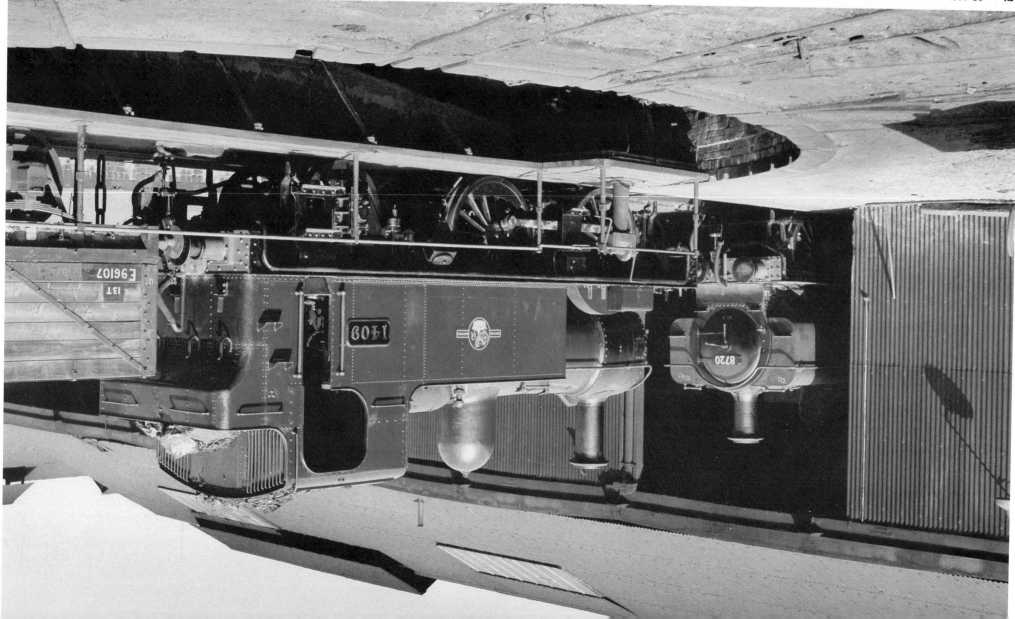

Plate 70 (Above): No. 5057 *Earl Waldegrave* pulls out of Moreton-in-Marsh with the 19.00 Worcester to Paddington express. To the rear of the signal box, the line to Shipston on Stour can be seen leading off to the right.

14th May 1960

Plate 71 (Below): An excursion from Paddington attracted a lot of attention when it was found to be hauled by the new No. 92220 *Evening Star*, just two months after its naming ceremony. It is seen leaving Stratford-upon-Avon heading south to Honeybourne Junction where it would join the Worcester-Oxford-London line for the remainder of the journey.

19th May 1960

Plate 72: An 0-6-2T, No. 5679, pilots No. 4093 *Dunster Castle* up the steep incline to Cockett Tunnel with a westbound train. This was only a short distance from Swansea, and it is surprising, when looking back, how much waste ground there was alongside the railway lines 26 years ago.

21st May 1960

Plate 73: The 'Cambrian Coast Express' blasts out of Harbury Tunnel on its way to London with No. 6000 *King George V* making a fine exhaust. To get one's BR walking permit renewed each year, one had to submit some sample photographs taken the previous year. I sent this one among my selection, completely forgetting it said in small print 'not at track level in cuttings'. A number of letters were required to put that mistake right!

28th May 1960

Plate 74 (Above): Following the 'Cambian Coast Express' 2-6-0 No. 7315 came out of the tunnel with a mixed goods train, including a double-deck car transporter wagon containing new Jaguar cars from Coventry. Being next to the locomotive they must have been filthy when they got to the end of the journey.

28th May 1960

Plate 75 (Below): With the well-known gasometers making an obvious background, 2-8-2T No. 7247 takes a freight out of Stratford-upon-Avon and, after a short downhill stretch, will begin the climb up to Wilmcote at 1 in 75.

7th June 1960

Plate 76: It is unusual to see pictures taken in Sonning Cutting from the north side of the tracks, but, in this case, with the sun head-on, there is just enough light to reflect off the coaches of the 'down' 'Cheltenham Spa Express' hauled by No. 7000 *Viscount Portal.*

2nd August 1960

Plate 77: A line of engines awaiting scrap in the Concentration Yard at Swindon Works which includes three 'Dukedogs'. The line-up includes Nos. 9496, 9018, 9015, 2264, 9004, 2842, 6300 and 2837.

7th August 1960

Plate 78 (Above): No. 5012 *Berry Pomeroy Castle* climbs slowly up Hatton Bank with a Saturday Bournemouth to Birkenhead train. The coaches are BR, and former Great Western and London North Eastern.

13th August 1960

Plate 79 (Below): The 'down' 'South Wales Pullman' passes Ebbw Junction signal box, Newport, hauled by No. 5006 *Tregenna Castle* with Ebbw Junction Shed just off the left-hand edge of the picture.

26th August 1960

Plate 80 (Above): Both the crew are watching the road ahead as they approach the tunnel to the west of Newport Station. A 2-8-0T, No. 5233, is just above the ATC ramp with the gib of a very substantial crane in the background.

26th August 1960

Plate 81 (Below): Shrewsbury Shed for Western and Midland Region engines is just this side of the gasometer, in the background, and a short freight is held at the signals. No. 7025 *Sudeley Castle* will shortly be starting the climb to Church Stretton with a Manchester to Plymouth express.

2nd September 1960

Plate 82 (Above): No. 7026 *Tenby Castle* with the 'down' 'Cornishman' is just about to pass over the new junction put in to enable freight trains to reach Banbury from the south-west, a shorter route than via Hatton. At the signals you can see 2-8-0 No. 2834 waiting to take the new curve to Stratford-upon-Avon Old Town Station.

11th November 1960

Plate 83 (Below): And now the 2-8-0 will soon join the SMJR for the climb up to Goldicote and over the single line to Fenny Compton, where it may turn south on to the main line for Banbury, or continue on to the Great Central line at Woodford Halse.

11th November 1960

Plate 84 (Above): The 'down' 'Cambrian Coast Express' has just passed Hatton North Junction, and will pass under the elegant brick-arch road bridge at Shrewley. No. 6000 *King George V* was a regular performer on this train and became a firm favourite.

12th November 1960

Plate 85 (Below): A 2-10-0, No. 92249, heads out of Stratford-upon-Avon with a freight for the Banbury area. The train has just passed through the Old Town Station and crosses the flooded River Avon on the SMJR line to Fenny Compton. In the background is the large grain silo which is a landmark in this part of the town.

5th December 1960

Plate 86: I had a splendid day's photography on the main line to the west of Didcot with the sun out all day, but it was bitterly cold. No. 5051 *Earl Bathhurst* hauls the 'down' 'Pembroke Coast Express' and looks almost as clean as it does today where it is in preservation at the Didcot Railway Centre.

27th December 1970

Plate 87: A broadside view of No. 5020 *Trematon Castle* with an 'up' express from Weston-super-Mare. The driver has spotted me standing in the middle of the field.

27th December 1960

Plate 88 (Above): The 'up' 'Cheltenham Spa Express' with No. 5017 *The Gloucestershire Regiment* at its head has just shut off steam as it approaches Didcot.

27th December 1960

Plate 89 (Below): Four days later, with more brilliant sun, it is back to Didcot again where 2-8-0 No. 2853 is seen passing through the station with a 'down' freight train.

31st December 1960

Plate 90 (Above): I took a large number of photographs in 'A' Shop at Swindon Works over the years, but this does not show how cold it was on a Sunday afternoon. No. 6938 *Corndean Hall*, No. 4098 *Kidwelly Castle* and No. 6022 *King Edward III* are in various stages of overhaul.

7th January 1961

Plate 91 (Below): A 2-6-2T, No. 5101, has just passed through Hatton Station with a freight for the Birmingham area. The lines to the right lead off for Stratford-upon-Avon and, between the arch of the road bridge, you can see the station signal box.

21st January 1961

Plate 94 (Above): In the evening, No. 7923 *Speke Hall* leaves Stratford-upon-Avon with a returning excursion to Pitsea, in Essex. A local goods train approaches the station behind 2-6-2T No. 4155.

8th June 1961

Plate 95 (Below): A 2-6-0, No. 6368, pilots No. 6803 *Bucklebury Grange* out of Chipping Campden Tunnel with a train of pigeons from Glasgow. It makes a rather unbelievable caption to write in 1986, and where today do you see such well-burnt grass on the embankments.

23rd June 1961

Plate 96: 'Black Five' No. 45447 and No. 6917 *Oldlands Hall* have a friendly race between Cheltenham and Gloucester, and are seen approaching Churchdown. At this point, the Birmingham to Bristol ex-LMS line ran side by side with the ex-GWR line. Both trains stopped at the two stations in Cheltenham and, being timed to leave at the same time, often converged as they were accelerating south. It became a spectacular bit of fun if the trains were on time and with the right crew. On this occasion the 'Black Five' is leading by half a length, but the Tyseley crew, on the Wolverhampton to Ilfracombe train, are pushing hard to catch up.

12th August 1961

Plate 97: No. 7808 Cookham Manor, on the returning Stephenson Locomotive Society special train, awaits its railway enthusiast passengers to finish taking photographs. This was the farewell to the Midland & South West Junction line between Cheltenham and Andover. The train will be leaving Ludgershall for Marlborough, and behind the signal box would be the branch to Tidworth.

10th September 1961

Plate 98 (Above): The large water tank on the skyline to the left of the picture supplies the village of Harbury with its water supply. No. 5072 *Hurricane* has just passed through the tunnel in the centre of Harbury Cutting with the 16.00 Birmingham (Snow Hill) to Paddington express.

18th September 1961

Plate 99 (Below): After following the Talyllyn special train through to Towyn the day before, it was an early start to visit some of the South Wales sheds. This picture was taken in the late afternoon on Cardiff (Canton) Shed — rather like looking for the Cuneo mouse one could play hunt the shovel. There are three in various stages of disrepair lying on the ground.

1st October 1961

Plate 100 (Above): Warwick gasworks is off the picture to the left and had its own narrow gauge system fed from the siding filled with wagons. No. 6020 *King Henry IV* is just about to pass under the Cape Road Bridge on the descent from Hatton to Warwick. The train will be the 11.35 Wolverhampton to Paddington express.

12th October 1961

Plate 101 (Below): No. 7004 *Eastnor Castle* climbs up towards Chipping Campden Tunnel with the 10.05 Hereford to Paddington express. A long section of the line leading up to the tunnel was overlooked by trees, giving problems with the shadows at this time of year. However, the trains working hard on the gradient looked and sounded magnificent as they came into sight with the shaft of sunlight flashing through the trees on to the copper and brass.

28th October 1961

Plate 102 (Above): Collett 0-6-0 No. 2211 has just arrived at Leamington Spa (General) Station with the 08.43 from Stratford-upon-Avon, and takes away the empty stock to the carriage sidings. The locomotive had not long been painted in lined-out green livery and it looks as if the cleaners at Leamington Shed were making an effort to keep it looking nice.

8th November 1961

Plate 103 (Below): As I lived at Stratford-upon-Avon, it was inevitable that many of my pictures were taken on the Worcester line, and here is another train having just passed through Honeybourne and on the climb near Mickleton. No. 7010 *Avondale Castle* hauls the 12.05 Hereford to Paddington.

9th November 1961

Plate 104: This scene is a little nearer Honeybourne Station, and shows No. 5076 *Gladiator* with the 09.17 Great Malvern to Paddington train. The lines to the right go off to join the Stratford-upon-Avon and Cheltenham route. With both signals off, there is a train due on the 'down' main line behind me and a train from the Stratford line which is signalled into the bay platform.

11th February 1962

Plate 105: A 4-4-0 'Dukedog' No. 9017, having been purchased from BR for private preservation, travelled under its own steam to the Bluebell Railway. It is seen here in Leamington Spa (General) Station.

14th February 1962

Plate 106 (Above): A 2-8-0, No. 3800, passes Fosse box, between Leamington Spa and Southam Road and Harbury Stations. There was a bitter north wind blowing so I took shelter in the signal box and shared the signalman's view of this train passing his box.

14th February 1962

Plate 107 (Below): This scene has appeared more than once in the book but it was surprising the variety of locomotive types used for such a mundane working. In this case it is a Tyseley-based engine, 0-6-2T No. 5658, and is seen leaving Stratford-upon-Avon with the 08.43 to Leamington Spa.

7th March 1962

Plate 108 (Above): The new Warwick by-pass is just out of the picture to the right and today this is a favourite spot to photograph the Sunday steam specials from London to Stratford-upon-Avon. No. 6000 King George V hauls the 'down' 'Inter-City' up the early stages of Hatton Bank.

16th March 1962

Plate 109 (Below): Another picture of the 'down' 'Inter-City', but near the summit of Hatton Bank hauled by No. 6026 King John, and without the usual reporting numbers on the smokebox door. What a mixture of liveries for the coaches — some in chocolate and cream others in maroon.

13th April 1962

Plate 110 (Above): A 2-10-0, No. 92211, heads a train of 24 empty oil tanks back to the refinery at Fawley, near Southampton. The train is just approaching the site of Littleton & Badsey Station, and this was a regular working for the BR 9Fs.

10th May 1962

Plate 111 (Below): The 17.00 Banbury to Princes Risborough local train pauses at Kings Sutton Station hauled by 0-4-2T No. 1440. This station, with its fascinating buildings, was well-maintained, together with the gardens. Note the gas lights, and particularly those on the footbridge.

15th May 1962

Plate 112: Shortly afterwards, No. 6017 *King Edward IV* storms through the station with the 'up' 'Inter-City' express. Two months prior to this picture being taken, it had been announced that all the 'Kings' would be withdrawn by the autumn, and the Western class diesels took over.

15th May 1962

Plate 113: No. 7026 *Tenby Castle* pulls out of Stratford-upon-Avon Station with 'The Cornishman' on its way to Wolverhampton. It had already been decided that the train would be replaced at the end of the summer season on 7th September. A diesel-hauled train would take its place running down the Midland main line from Birmingham. This was the start of the decline in passenger services through Stratford-upon-Avon.

22nd May 1962

Plate 114: I spent a day in the London area watching the arrivals and departures outside Paddington. In this case No. 7031 *Cromwell's Castle* is setting out with the 13.15 Paddington to Worcester train and is passing Ranelagh Bridge Yard.

18th August 1962

Plate 115: No. 7027 *Thornbury Castle* pulls out of Evesham Station with the 'up' 'Cathedrals Express' as 2-8-0 No. 3809 approaches with an oil train. In the distance, the Midland Region line from Evesham to Redditch crosses over the Western Region line.

22nd September 1962

Plate 116 (Above): At the relatively new South Yard at Honeybourne, No. 7915 *Mere Hall*; on a southbound freight, heads for Toddington and Cheltenham. A 2-10-0, No. 92236, has just taken water, and an unidentified Austerity is in the background.

24th December 1962

Plate 117 (Below): No. 7929 *Wyke Hall* and No. 72008 *Clan Macleod* leave Oxley with a special train organised by the Derbyshire Locomotive Society. The train ran from Leeds to Tyseley Shed with the 'Clan' class locomotive and Tyseley supplied the 'Hall' to pilot it all the way back to Crewe, with visits to Wolverhampton Works and Stafford Road and Oxley sheds.

24th March 1963

Plate 118 (Above): With a very stormy sky, and just a glimpse of the sun, No. 1005 *County of Devon* approaches Church Stretton with a Manchester to Plymouth express.

30th March 1963

Plate 119 (Below): A 2-8-0, No. 3818, toils up the bank having just come through Chipping Campden Tunnel with a freight train. This was a perfect setting for watching and listening to trains. There was no road traffic noises and, being surrounded by trees, was like sitting in a nature reserve. The continual song of the birds was only broken by the passing of the trains.

6th April 1963

Plate 120 (Below): An 0-6-0PT, No. 4614, crosses the River Avon with a local train from Ashchurch to Evesham. Underneath the bridge you can just see the main Western Region line curving towards Worcester. The bridge has since been dismantled.

4th May 1963

Plate 121 (Below): I had an official footplate ride from Evesham to Paddington and back with a special request that it should be a 'Castle'. Worcester Shed turned out No. 7025 *Sudeley Castle* for the trip and here we are about to pass the locomotive shed at Oxford.

22nd May 1963

Plate 122 (Above): Having arrived in the morning with the 'Cathedrals Express' I returned this time behind No. 7027 *Thornbury Castle*, and this is the approach to the south end of Oxford Station. No. 7920 *Coney Hall* has just arrived with the 15.10 Worcester to Paddington train, and it looks as if the two trainspotters on the platform, with caps and bags, have just come out of school.

22nd May 1963

Plate 123 (Below): No. 6847 *Tidmarsh Grange* has just passed the summit of the northbound climb from Abergavenny with a Cardiff to Blackpool train. It is interesting to visit Llanvihangel today since nothing remains to show that a station ever existed there.

27th July 1963

Plate 124 (Above): This was another splendid spot for photography on the climb from Honeybourne to Chipping Campden Tunnel. Again it is the empty oil tanks going back to Fawley, but this time hauled by 2-8-0 No. 2899.

1st February 1964

Plate 125 (Below): Down in the Stroud Valley, an 0-4-2T and auto coach No. W230W leaves St. Mary's Crossing Halt with a local train from Gloucester to Chalford.

19th May 1964

Plate 126: No. 5983 *Henley Hall* approaches Hatton Station with a 'down' freight including LBSCR 'Terrier' tank No. 32662, being taken to the Butlin's Holiday Camp at Ayr, in Scotland, and now at Bressingham Hall, Diss, Norfolk.

26th September 1964